EXPLORING DINOSAURS & PREHISTORIC CREATURES

MEGATHERIUM

By Susan H. Gray

THE CHILD'S WORLD®
CHANHASSEN, MINNESOTA

Published in the United States of America by The Child's World®
PO Box 326, Chanhassen, MN 55317-0326
800-599-READ
www.childsworld.com

Content Adviser:
Brian Huber, PhD,
Curator, Department
of Paleobiology,
Smithsonian
National Museum
of Natural History,
Washington DC

Photo Credits: Illustration by Karen Carr: 16; Kevin Schafer/Corbis: 6; Michael &
Patricia Fogden/Corbis: 7, 8, 14; Hubert Stadler/Corbis: 21; Bettmann/Corbis: 22, 23;
The Field Museum, GEO84608c, Photographer Ron Testa: 15; Mike Fredericks: 4;
John Chiasson/Liaison/Getty Images: 18; Daniel LeClair/Getty Images: 19; The
Natural History Museum, London: 5, 9, 11, 13, 17; Tom McHugh/Photo Researchers,
Inc.: 10, 25; Tom McHugh/Field Museum Chicago/Photo Researchers, Inc.: 27;
Chip Clark/National Museum of Natural History/Smithsonian Institution: 20;
Ken Lucas/Visuals Unlimited: 12.

The Child's World®: Mary Berendes, Publishing Director

Editorial Directions, Inc.: E. Russell Primm, Editorial Director; Pam Rosenberg,
Line Editor; Katie Marsico, Associate Editor; Matthew Messbarger, Editorial Assistant;
Susan Hindman, Copy Editor; Melissa McDaniel, Proofreader; Tim Griffin/IndexServ,
Indexer; Olivia Nellums, Fact Checker; Dawn Friedman, Photo Researcher; Linda
S. Koutris, Photo Selector

Original cover art by Todd Marshall

The Design Lab: Kathleen Petelinsek, Design and Page Production

Library of Congress Cataloging-in-Publication Data
Gray, Susan Heinrichs.
  Megatherium / by Susan H. Gray.
    p. cm. — (Exploring dinosaurs & prehistoric creatures)
  Includes index.
  ISBN 1-59296-410-9 (lib. bd. : alk. paper) 1. Megatherium—Juvenile literature. I.
Title.
  QE882.E2G73 2005
  569'.31—dc22   2004018076

TABLE OF CONTENTS

CHAPTER ONE

HITTING THE SPOT

Megatherium (MEG-uh-THEER-ee-um) had a terrible itch on her back. She sat down and tried to scratch it with one of her feet. But even with claws the size of bananas, she couldn't quite reach the spot. She awkwardly bent an arm backward, straining for the bothersome itch. But that didn't do the trick either.

Then she spied a cluster of pine trees in the distance. *Megatherium* heaved her huge body up onto all four feet and

Megatherium *had huge claws, but would still have had a hard time scratching an itch on its back.*

headed slowly toward the trees.

Once she reached the grove, she

rose up on her hind legs. She

became taller and taller until she

reached her full two-story height.

Still moving slowly, she approached

the closest tree. Its bark was rough

and scaly—perfect for scratching

an itchy back.

Giant Megatherium *was able to walk on its hind legs, as well as on all fours.*

Megatherium backed up to the tree and leaned against its trunk.

Then she scrubbed back and forth against the rough bark. That really

hit the spot. *Megatherium* closed her eyes and kept scratching. After a

few minutes, the huge sloth (SLAWTH) was satisfied. She dropped to

four feet again and slowly walked away.

CHAPTER TWO

WHAT ARE SLOTHS?

Sloths are **mammals** that are herbivores (URB-ih-vorz), or plant eaters. There are two main kinds of sloths—tree sloths, which are living today, and ground sloths, which are **extinct.**

Modern-day sloths live in Central and South America. They spend almost their entire lives in trees, feeding on leaves. Tree sloths have large stomachs that slowly digest their leafy meals. The animals have furry

Megatherium *died out about 10,000 years ago and was an ancestor of the modern-day tree sloth (shown here).*

Like most of its relatives, this brown-throated three-toed sloth rarely leaves the trees. Not only do sloths find most of their food in the treetops, but they are also in greater danger from **predators** *while on the forest floor.*

bodies, long legs, and strong arms. They also have long claws on their hands, which they use for climbing.

Tree sloths are known for their extremely slow movements. In fact, some spend much of their time completely still, moving only when absolutely necessary. The word *sloth* actually means "laziness."

Sloths have two layers of fur. An outer layer is long and shaggy.

It covers a short, dense coat underneath. The long hairs of the outer

coat have many fine cracks in them. **Microscopic** plants called

algae (AL-jee) live in the cracks.

During very wet or rainy periods, the

algae grow so much that the sloths

look like they have green fur!

There are two kinds of tree sloths

living today—three-toed sloths and

two-toed sloths. Three-toed sloths

have three long claws on each hand.

These animals grow to be about

9 pounds (4 kilograms) as adults,

which is almost as heavy as a

Most sloths are brown or gray, but this one is green! The algae that grow on a sloth's fur helps the animal blend in with its surroundings.

Prehistoric sloths often weighed more than 500 times as much as their modern-day relatives.

house cat. The two-toed sloths have two long claws on each hand and

can weigh up to 18 pounds (8 kg). Although sloths don't move fast or

often, they are more active at night than during the day. Modern sloths

tend to be **nocturnal** animals.

Though many ground sloths were as small as modern sloths,

some reached incredible sizes. Ground sloths spent much of their time

grazing on grasses and short plants or gnawing the leaves of bushes and

By walking with their claws off the ground, prehistoric sloths were able to keep them sharp. Some scientists believe the animals may have used these claws to hook plant matter high up in the trees.

trees. Like their tree-dwelling cousins, ground sloths had long claws on their hands. They also had quite lengthy claws on their feet.

Ground sloths had an interesting way of walking. Sometimes they walked on all four feet, and sometimes they walked in an upright position. Either way, they always walked on the outer edges of their feet. The soles of their feet faced each other. When they walked on all fours, their hands rested on their wrists or knuckles. By walking this way, ground sloths kept their claws off the ground. This helped the claws stay long and sharp.

CHAPTER THREE

WHAT WAS *MEGATHERIUM*?

Megatherium was one of the biggest ground sloths that ever existed. Its name means "great beast." *Megatherium* lived in South America and possibly in parts of North America. Scientists believe that ground sloths first appeared about 35 million years ago and that *Megatherium* appeared about 2 million years ago. It became extinct about 10,000 years ago.

When on its hind legs, Megatherium *stood three to four times as tall as the average human being.*

The "great beast" grew to a length of about 20 feet (6 meters) and weighed between 3 and 4 tons. It was about the same size as an

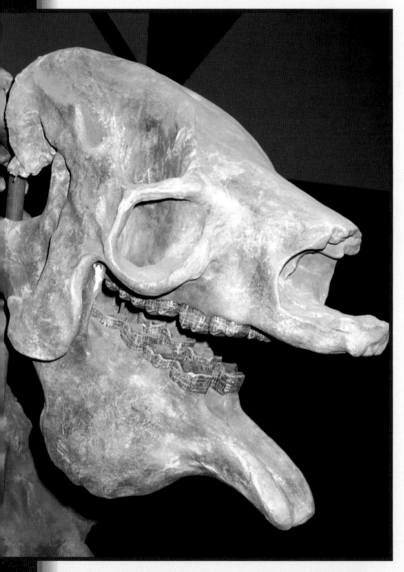

elephant. Like other ground sloths, it walked on either two or four feet. We know this because its footprints have been found in South America.

Megatherium was covered in a thick, shaggy coat. It had a small head for its body and peglike teeth for grinding plant material. The animal had

Scientists can tell Megatherium *was a plant eater by studying its peglike teeth. If the animal had been a meat eater, its teeth would have been sharper and more curved.*

narrow shoulders, strong arms, and three long, curved claws on each hand. The sloth used its claws to hook leafy branches and fruit and draw them toward its mouth. *Megatherium* also used its claws to strip bark from trees. It would then

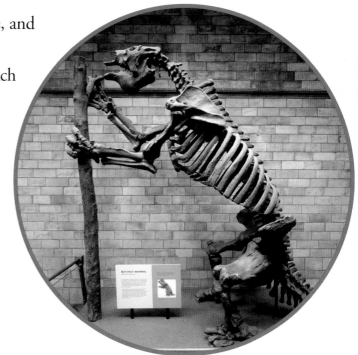

Like many other prehistoric creatures that walked on two legs, Megatherium *used its thick tail for balance.*

curl its long tongue around the strips and pull them into its mouth.

The sloth's hips and back legs were massive. They had to be huge in order to support the beast when it stood upright. The tail was not long, but it was thick and heavy. The sloth probably used it for balance. Even when standing upright, *Megatherium* rested on the outer edges of its feet, always protecting those claws.

DON'T BE FOOLED!

Megatherium was a huge, meaty animal. It had no sharp teeth. It had no spikes on its head or tail. It was too big and bulky to climb a tree. It was probably just as slow moving as its modern-day cousins. Surely predators saw the beast as an easy meal—something they could take down without a fight.

But they probably got a nasty surprise. Modern-day sloths can move rather quickly when threatened. Some will snort and make hissing sounds when disturbed. Some

will viciously snap at attackers. And, if really alarmed, sloths will strike at other animals, slashing them with their sharp claws.

Megatherium was enormous. It was big enough to make many predators think twice before attacking. Even though its teeth were not sharp, a quick snap of its jaws would have scared some enemies away. And a sudden swipe with those mega-claws would have sent others running. There were probably a few pred-ators that were fooled by *Megatherium*'s slow-moving ways. But they weren't fooled twice!

CHAPTER FOUR

HOW DID *MEGATHERIUM* SPEND ITS TIME?

Megatherium had a huge body, so it needed to eat large amounts of food. It had a small mouth, so it couldn't gulp down big bites. It probably moved slowly, so it wasn't a fast

Giant ground sloths probably used their huge tongues to help collect plant matter.

eater. Therefore,

Megatherium probably

spent a tremendous amount

of time just eating. Scientists

have found hundreds of

ground sloth droppings in

the caves of North and

South America. The drop-

pings show that ground

sloths ate all sorts of

In addition to collecting fossilized bones and skeletons, scientists also study the hardened droppings of prehistoric animals. These remains provide clues about what an animal ate and how its digestive system worked.

plants—grasses, lilies, grapes, mint, and even cactuses.

    Megatherium digested its food while it slept. Plant material

is difficult to digest, so plant eaters have very long digestive

systems. It takes a long time for food to pass through them.

Many herbivores have big bellies to hold their long digestive tracts.

This was surely the case with *Megatherium*. It had a big rib cage

and wide hips to support that belly.

Like Megatherium, *plant-eating* Triceratops *(try-SEHR-uh-tops)*
had a huge belly that contained a long digestive tract.

The fossilized remains of a ground sloth's rib cage help confirm that these animals were plant eaters. The large rib cage helped support a big belly, which in turn contained the type of digestive tract typically found in most herbivores.

Scientists can't say for certain whether *Megatherium* was active in the daytime or at night. The animal may have found protection in caves and slept there. It was much too big to find safety in trees. When it was awake, an adult *Megatherium* probably spent time eating, searching for a mate, or caring for its young.

CHAPTER FIVE

SOME DIFFERENT GROUND SLOTHS

Megatherium was not the only ground sloth that existed in prehistoric times. Scientists have discovered that others lived in North, Central, and South America, and even in the Caribbean Islands. The smallest ground sloths were about the size of modern-day tree sloths. The largest were the elephant-sized *Megatherium* and *Eremotherium* (EH-reh-moh-THEER-ee-um).

Scientists have discovered several Eremotherium **fossils** *in southern states such as Florida.*

Eremotherium was a close relative of *Megatherium*. At one time, it probably lived only in South America. Then it slowly moved north. The animal eventual-

Mylodon *was smaller than both* Eremotherium *and* Megatherium *and was about the size of a modern-day ox.*

ly spread throughout what is now the southern United States, where bushes and trees were plentiful for feeding.

Mylodon (MY-loh-don) was a smaller ground sloth that ate grasses and possibly roots. Both *Mylodon* and *Eremotherium* had tough skin with a layer of small bony plates just beneath it. The plates protected the animals from attacks by predators.

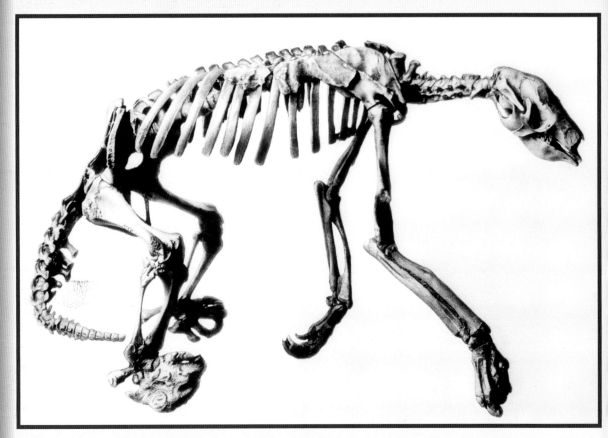

Nothrotheriops *was one of the smallest North American ground sloths.*

At about 6 to 7 feet (1.8 to 2 m) in height, *Megalonyx* (MEG-uh-LAW-nix) was the size of a bear. Scientists have found its claws and bones in Mexico, the United States, and Canada.

Nothrotheriops (NO-throw-THEER-ee-ops) was covered with long brown fur. It lived in caves in North America. *Nothrotheriops* may even have had algae growing on its fur, just like the tree sloths of today.

THE PRESIDENT AND THE GROUND SLOTH

Thomas Jefferson (below) was the third president of the United States and a man with many interests. He worked in the government and wrote the Declaration of Independence. Planning building projects was another one of his interests, and he designed his own home. Involved in education, he helped start a university. He was also quite interested in science.

In Jefferson's day, people did not know about dinosaurs or other animals that had become extinct. Whenever scientists found mysterious fossils, they figured the remains came from animals that were still around. They believed that if they just looked hard enough, they would find those animals living somewhere.

So in the 1790s, when an unusual fossil was

discovered in a Virginia cave, everyone thought it was from an animal that still existed. The specimen was a huge claw. Jefferson, who lived in Virginia, became interested immediately. He studied the claw and decided it came from some kind of lion. Jefferson was so sure of this that he wrote a paper about it and named the lion *Megalonyx,* meaning "great claw." Jefferson even spoke to the American explorer Meriwether Lewis about the lion. He told Lewis to look for it wherever his travels took him.

Lewis never found the lion because there was no lion to be found. As it turned out, the great claw was from a giant ground sloth that had become extinct. At the time of the claw's discovery, no one had even heard of giant ground sloths, and certainly no one believed in extinction.

Still, Jefferson will always be linked with the beast. Twenty-five years after he wrote his lion paper, a French scientist gave the animal a new name. He knew it was a ground sloth, and he called it *Megalonyx jeffersonii* (JEFF-er-SO-nee-eye), meaning "Jefferson's great claw." Today, the animal is known as Jefferson's ground sloth.

CHAPTER SIX

GROUND SLOTHS THROUGH TIME

The oldest fossils of ground sloths are from South America.

The sloths probably took millions of years to spread

throughout the **continent.** In time, they slowly made their way

Ground sloths existed on Earth for 35 million years and lived on two different continents.

to North America, where they spread into what are now Mexico, the United States, and Canada.

During their 35 million years on Earth, ground sloths endured several major changes in climate. They survived warm, humid periods and cold, dry periods. The final stretch of time when the sloths lived is called the Pleistocene **epoch** (PLY-stoh-seen EP-uk). During this time period, great ice sheets formed over parts of Earth's surface. Many places were quite cold. Other areas were cool, but not freezing. With their shaggy fur, the ground sloths were well suited to the cool temperatures.

About 10,000 years ago, Earth began to warm up, and human beings began to spread into new areas. Perhaps these events brought about the giant creatures' extinction. Perhaps predators, decreasing food supplies, or other factors caused their

Prehistoric humans may have contributed to Megatherium's *downfall through overhunting.*

disappearance. We will probably never know exactly why the giant

ground sloths died out. But we do know that *Megatherium* was one

of the last to go.

Glossary

continent (KON-tuh-nuhnt)
A continent is one of Earth's large landmasses. Ground sloths lived on two continents.

epoch (EP-uhk) An epoch is a time period in which important events took place. The Pleistocene epoch was the last stretch of time when prehistoric ground sloths lived.

extinct (ek-STINGKT) Something that is extinct has died out and is no longer in existence. *Megatherium* is now extinct.

fossils (FOSS-uhlz) Fossils are things that are left behind by ancient plants or animals, such as skeletons or footprints. The oldest ground sloth fossils were found in South America.

mammals (MAM-uhlz) Mammals are animals that are warm-blooded, have backbones and hair (or fur), and feed their young milk made by the bodies of the mothers. Sloths are mammals.

microscopic (mye-kruh-SKOP-ik) Something that is microscopic is so small that it cannot be seen without a special tool called a microscope. Algae are microscopic.

nocturnal (nok-TUR-nuhl) Animals that are nocturnal are active at night. Modern-day sloths are nocturnal.

predators (PRED-uh-torz) Predators are animals that hunt and eat other animals. *Megatherium*'s enormous size helped to keep predators away.

specimen (SPESS-uh-muhn) A specimen is a sample that is used to represent an entire group. In the 1790s, a fossil specimen of a giant ground sloth was found in a Virginia cave.

Did You Know?

▸ *Megatherium* is related not only to modern-day tree sloths but also to armadillos and anteaters. All have extra joints in their backbones—joints that no other mammals have.

▸ The teeth of sloths grow continuously. They have no enamel, which is the hard outer covering of teeth.

▸ Dried remains of ancient ground sloths have been found in caves in the southwestern United States. The remains include pieces of muscle, bone, and hairy skin.

How to Learn More

AT THE LIBRARY

Lambert, David, Darren Naish, and Liz Wyse.
Dinosaur Encyclopedia: From Dinosaurs to the Dawn of Man.
New York: Dorling Kindersley, 2001.

Palmer, Douglas, and Barry Cox (editor).
The Simon & Schuster Encyclopedia of Dinosaurs & Prehistoric Creatures: A Visual Who's Who of Prehistoric Life.
New York: Simon & Schuster, 1999.

ON THE WEB

Visit our home page for lots of links about *Megatherium*:
http://www.childsworld.com/links.html
NOTE TO PARENTS, TEACHERS, AND LIBRARIANS: We routinely verify our Web links
to make sure they're safe, active sites—so encourage your readers to check them out!

PLACES TO VISIT OR CONTACT

AMERICAN MUSEUM OF
NATURAL HISTORY
To view many fossils of extinct animals
Central Park West at 79th Street
New York, NY 10024-5192
212/769-5100

CARNEGIE MUSEUM OF
NATURAL HISTORY
To view the fossils of many extinct animals
4400 Forbes Avenue
Pittsburgh, PA 15213
412/622-3131

SAN ANTONIO ZOO
*To see tree sloths, the living relatives
of ancient* Megatherium
3903 N. St. Mary's Street
San Antonio, TX 78212
210/734-7184

SMITHSONIAN NATIONAL MUSEUM
OF NATURAL HISTORY
*To see several fossil exhibits and take
special behind-the-scenes tours*
10th Street and Constitution Avenue NW
Washington, DC 20560-0166
202/357-2700

The Geologic Time Scale

CAMBRIAN PERIOD

Date: 540 million to 505 million years ago
Most major animal groups appeared by the end of this period. Trilobites were common and algae became more diversified.

ORDOVICIAN PERIOD

Date: 505 million to 440 million years ago
Marine life became more diversified. Crinoids and blastoids appeared, as did corals and primitive fish. The first land plants appeared. The climate changed greatly during this period—it began as warm and moist, but temperatures ultimately dropped. Huge glaciers formed, causing sea levels to fall.

SILURIAN PERIOD

Date: 440 million to 410 million years ago
Glaciers melted, sea levels rose, and Earth's climate became more stable. Plants with vascular systems developed. This means they had parts that helped them to conduct food and water.

DEVONIAN PERIOD

Date: 410 million to 360 million years ago
Fish became more diverse, as did land plants. The first trees and forests appeared at this time, and the earliest seed-bearing plants began to grow. The first land-living vertebrates and insects appeared. Fossils also reveal evidence of the first ammonoids and amphibians. The climate was warm and mild.

CARBONIFEROUS PERIOD

Date: 360 million to 286 million years ago
The climate was warm and humid, but cooled toward the end of the period. Coal swamps dotted the landscape, as did a multitude of ferns. The earliest reptiles appeared on Earth. Pelycosaurs such as *Edaphosaurus* evolved toward the end of the Carboniferous period.

PERMIAN PERIOD

Date: 286 million to 248 million years ago
Algae, sponges, and corals were common on the ocean floor. Amphibians and reptiles were also prevalent at this time, as were seed-bearing plants and conifers. This period ended with the largest mass extinction on Earth. This may have been caused by volcanic activity or the formation of glaciers and the lowering of sea levels.

TRIASSIC PERIOD

Date: 248 million to 208 million years ago
The climate during this period was warm and dry. The first true mammals appeared, as did frogs, salamanders, and lizards. Evergreen trees made up much of the plant life. The first dinosaurs, including *Coelophysis*, existed on Earth. In the skies, pterosaurs became the earliest winged reptiles to take flight. In the seas, ichthyosaurs and plesiosaurs made their appearance.

JURASSIC PERIOD

Date: 208 million to 144 million years ago
The climate of the Jurassic period was warm and moist. The first birds appeared at this time, and plant life was more diverse and widespread. Although dinosaurs didn't even exist in the beginning of the Triassic period, they ruled Earth by Jurassic times. *Allosaurus, Apatosaurus, Archaeopteryx, Brachiosaurus, Compsognathus, Diplodocus, Ichthyosaurus, Plesiosaurus,* and *Stegosaurus* were just a few of the prehistoric creatures that lived during this period.

CRETACEOUS PERIOD

Date: 144 million to 65 million years ago
The climate of the Cretaceous period was fairly mild. Many modern plants developed, including those with flowers. With flowering plants came a greater diversity of insect life. Birds further developed into two types: flying and flightless. Prehistoric creatures such as *Ankylosaurus, Edmontosaurus, Iguanodon, Maiasaura, Oviraptor, Psittacosaurus, Spinosaurus, Triceratops, Troodon, Tyrannosaurus rex,* and *Velociraptor* all existed during this period. At the end of the Cretaceous period came a great mass extinction that wiped out the dinosaurs, along with many other groups of animals.

TERTIARY PERIOD

Date: 65 million to 1.8 million years ago
Mammals were extremely diversified at this time, and modern-day creatures such as horses, dogs, cats, bears, and whales developed.

QUATERNARY PERIOD

Date: 1.8 million years ago to today
Temperatures continued to drop during this period. Several periods of glacial development led to what is known as the Ice Age. Prehistoric creatures such as glyptodonts, mammoths, mastodons, *Megatherium,* and saber-toothed cats roamed Earth. A mass extinction of these animals occurred approximately 10,000 years ago. The first human beings evolved during the Quaternary period.

Index

About the Author

Susan H. Gray has bachelor's and master's degrees in zoology and has taught college-level courses in biology. She first fell in love with fossil hunting while studying paleontology in college. In her 25 years as an author, she has written many articles for scientists and researchers, and many science books for children. Susan enjoys gardening, traveling, and playing the piano. She and her husband, Michael, live in Cabot, Arkansas.